FOCUS ON ELEMENTARY
CHEMISTRY
3rd Edition

Rebecca W. Keller, PhD

REAL SCIENCE 4 Kids

Real Science-4-Kids

Illustrations: Janet Moneymaker

Focus On Elementary Chemistry Student Textbook—3rd Edition (softcover)
ISBN 978-1-941181-36-2

Published by Gravitas Publications Inc.
www.gravitaspublications.com
www.realscience4kids.com

GRAVITAS
PUBLICATIONS

Contents

Chapter 1 What Is Chemistry?

1.1 Introduction

Science is a way to study how things work. Science is made up of five different scientific subjects: chemistry, biology, physics, astronomy, and geology. These five subjects are the building blocks for all science.

In this chapter we will explore the building block called chemistry. Chemistry investigates what physical things are made of and the ways in which they change. Everything you can see, smell, or touch is made of "something." Scientists call this "something" matter. Chemistry is the study of matter.

1.2 History of Chemistry

A long time ago, students didn't study chemistry in school. Today, chemistry is an important part of all science, and students all over the globe study chemistry.

But where did we get chemistry?

Without knowing about chemistry, ancient people still did lots of chemistry. Ancient people used chemical processes every day.

A chemical process is any activity that involves some kind of chemistry.

For example, when ancient people treated animal furs so that they could be used as clothing, they were doing chemistry.

When ancient people created paints to draw pictures on walls, they were doing chemistry. And when ancient people made bowls or coins from metal, they were doing chemistry.

Ancient people did a lot of experimenting to learn about the world around them. Experimenting just means testing ideas and observing what happens.

For example, by experimenting, ancient people learned whether or not something would burn or melt. They learned if something tasted sweet or bitter. They learned that some things change color when added to other things. They even learned that some plants could be used as medicine. All of this is chemistry.

However, people didn't start thinking about chemistry as a science until the late 16th century. Around this same time, other scientific subjects, such as physics and astronomy, were also being developed. Also at this time, there were lots of people who did not do any experimenting at all, but just thought about things.

Thinking about how things work and doing experiments are two different ways to learn about the world.

In the late 16th century, thinkers began thinking about experimenting. Eventually thinking and doing were blended together, and these two ways of studying the world turned into what we call chemistry.

1.3 Modern Chemistry

Thinking about how the world works and doing experiments to observe how the world works are both important to modern chemistry.

We will see in Chapter 3 that matter is made of atoms. But atoms are so small that they can't be seen with our eyes. So if we can't see them with our eyes, how do we know they really exist?

Modern chemists do experiments to show that atoms exist. From these experiments they can learn a great deal about atoms. For example, by doing an experiment a chemist might find out how large an atom is, how fast it can move, or how heavy it is.

Modern chemists also think about atoms and make models to explain how atoms behave. A model is a good guess about how something works. Models can be created as writing, drawings, or computer programs, or they can be built from different materials. A model may not be completely true, but good models help chemists understand how things might work.

In Chapter 3 you will see a model for atoms. Each atom is drawn with a face and arms. Real atoms don't have arms, but that's OK. The models of atoms used in Chapter 3 will help you understand how atoms work.

1.4 Everyday Chemistry

You use chemistry every day, but you probably don't know it.

When you brush your teeth in the morning, chemicals in the toothpaste help clean your mouth. This is chemistry.

If you have a tummy ache, your mom might give you some medicine to make you feel better. This is chemistry.

If you want ice cream, your big sister might put gas in the car to drive you to the ice cream store. This is chemistry.

Even when you use watercolors to paint a picture, you are using chemistry.

Chemistry is everywhere! In this book you will learn more about chemistry and how we use chemistry every day.

1.5 Summary

○ Chemistry is the study of matter.

○ Chemistry is both thinking about how things work (making models) and doing experiments.

○ Chemistry happens every day, and we use chemistry in many different ways.

1.6 Some Things to Think About

○ When you are studying chemistry, what do you think you will be learning about?

○   Why do you think doing chemistry experiments is important?

○   What is your favorite type of model?

   Models of cars and toy cars

   Models of airplanes and toy airplanes

   Models of people and dolls

   Models of buildings and toy houses

   Models of the solar system and toy planets

   Other models and toys (What are they?)

○   How would you describe three activities you do every day that use chemistry?

Chapter 2 Chemist's Toolbox

2.1 Introduction

How do you study tiny atoms? How do you see small molecules? How can you measure, weigh, and monitor chemical reactions?

Today, chemists use a variety of tools to study atoms, molecules, and chemical reactions. The tools chemists use include special types of glass, metals, and equipment to study the smallest building blocks of matter. In this chapter we will take a look at some of these tools.

2.2 Brief History

The earliest chemists were called alchemists. Alchemists tried very hard to turn metals, such as lead, into gold. They never got it to work, but they did learn about chemical reactions. Alchemists were not true chemists as we know them today because alchemists did not use a scientific method. But alchemists learned a great deal about how different chemicals react with other chemicals.

Early chemistry tools and equipment used by alchemists were made of glass, clay, stone, and a variety of metals. One early chemistry tool called the alembic was used by early Greek and Arabic alchemists to make perfumes and medicines. Another early chemistry tool called the pelican was similar to the

alembic and was also used to purify materials for medicines, perfumes, and alcohol. Today, alembics and pelicans continue to be important tools in chemistry labs.

2.3 Basic Chemistry Tools

Chemists use many different kinds of tools and equipment. Most chemistry labs have both basic tools and advanced tools (instruments).

Chemists often need to measure the quantity of a liquid. A liquid is any pourable substance, such as water. You can't measure liquid water with a ruler, so you have to put it into a container that will help you measure how much you have.

For example, when you bake a cake, you use a measuring cup to measure liquids such as water, milk, and vegetable oil. A chemist uses a basic tool called a beaker in the same way as you use a measuring cup. Like a measuring cup, a beaker has lines on it showing how much liquid it contains, and it has a small spout

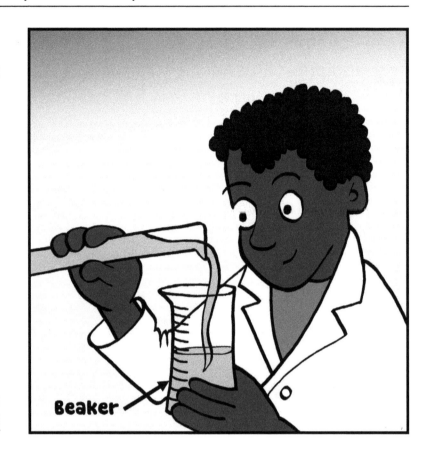

Beaker

for pouring. Beakers don't have a handle like a measuring cup, and the sides of beakers are straight up and down rather than being angled. In a chemistry lab, a beaker does the same job as a measuring cup.

Simple scales and balances are basic tools found in chemistry labs. To measure how much "stuff" there is, scales and balances are used. To find out how much of you there is, you would use a scale. When you go to the doctor's office, they have you step on a platform. They adjust some weights to show how much you weigh, or they read a number from a display. A scale is used to weigh you, just like a chemist uses a scale to weigh objects in the lab!

2.4 Advanced Chemistry Tools

All over the world there are many different types of chemistry labs studying different kinds of chemistry. Often you can find advanced tools (instruments) in these labs.

For example, a lab that is studying gases might use a gas chromatograph. A gas chromatograph is an instrument that can detect different types of gases in even very small amounts. A gas chromatograph has long tubes connected to a computer or a machine that draws graphs. The chemist puts a gas in one of the tubes, the gas chromatograph tests it, and the results are displayed on a computer or are printed out.

Many chemistry labs research ways to make new chemicals. Some of their experiments are quite complicated. For example, sometimes a chemistry experiment might require that little or no oxygen gas come in contact with the chemicals, so specialized equipment is used to keep the oxygen out. These experiments require advanced glassware of different sizes and shapes. Like the alembic and pelican, some of this glassware has funny names, such as an Erlenmeyer bulb or a Buchner flask!

It is not uncommon for chemists to make their own specialized tubes and glassware to use in specific experiments. In school, many young chemists learn how to blow, cut, and mold glass so they can create unique glassware for special experiments.

2.5 Summary

○ Chemists use a variety of basic tools and specialized advanced instruments to do experiments.

○ The early alchemists tried to turn lead into gold.

○ Some basic chemistry tools are beakers, scales, and balances.

○ Chemists sometimes make their own specialized glassware to use in experiments.

2.6 Some Things to Think About

○ What type of tool would you use to weigh a tablespoon of salt?

What type of tool would you use to weigh *you?*

○ What is your favorite smell?

Flowers? Baking bread? Cut grass? Printed ink a new book? Rain? Something else?

○ Do you think it would be easier to measure a glass full of water with a measuring cup or a teaspoon? Why?

○ If you worked in a chemistry lab what kind of chemistry tool do you think would be the most interesting to use?

Beakers and graduated flasks

Scales and balances

A gas chromatograph

An infrared spectrometer

An electron microscope

Chapter 3 Atoms

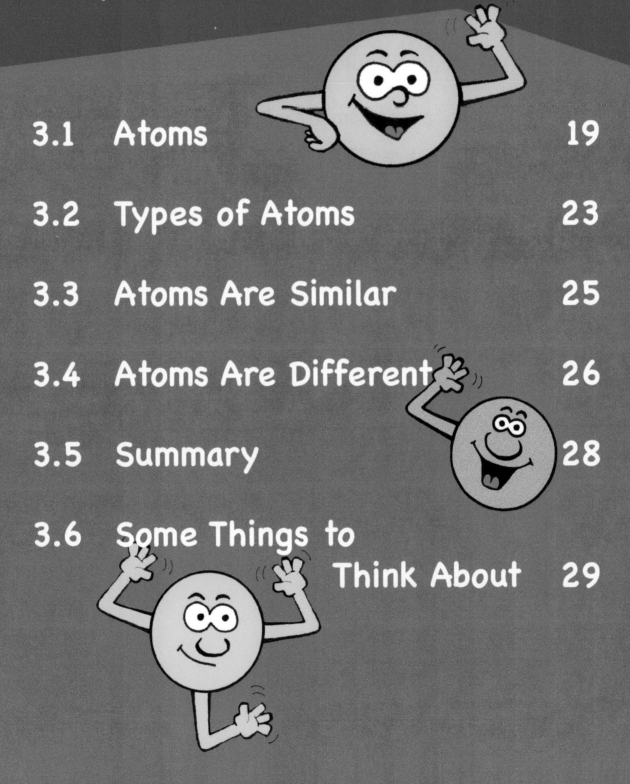

3.1 Atoms

Have you ever wondered if the Moon is really made of green cheese?

Have you ever thought the clouds might be made of cotton candy?

Have you ever wanted to know what makes carrots orange...

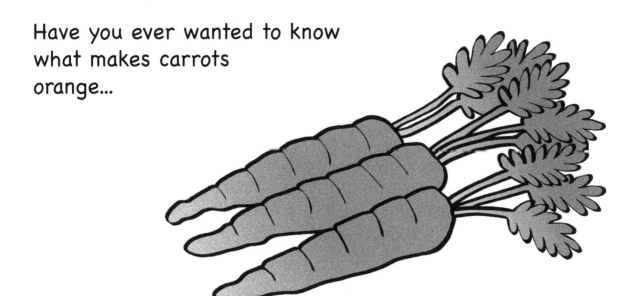

or peas green?

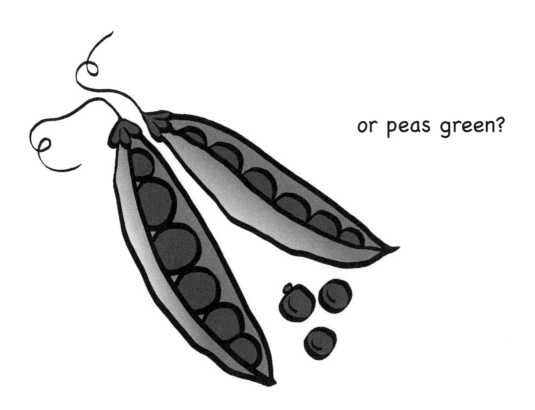

Have you ever wondered why brussels sprouts couldn't taste more like sweet cherries, or asparagus taste more like candy canes?

Everything around us has a different shape or flavor or color because everything around us is put together with different combinations of atoms. An atom is the smallest unit that makes up matter. Atoms can combine with one another in different groupings to make different substances.

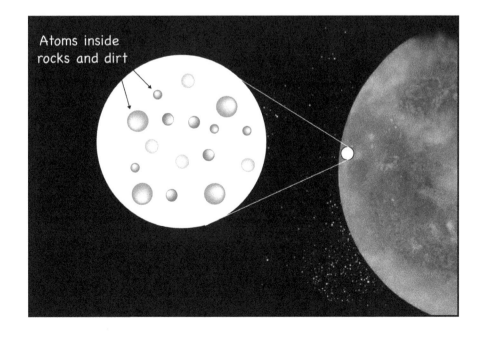

Atoms inside rocks and dirt

The Moon is not really made of green cheese. It is made of the kinds of atoms that are found in rocks and dirt.

Clouds are not made of cotton candy, but of the kinds of atoms that are found in air and water.

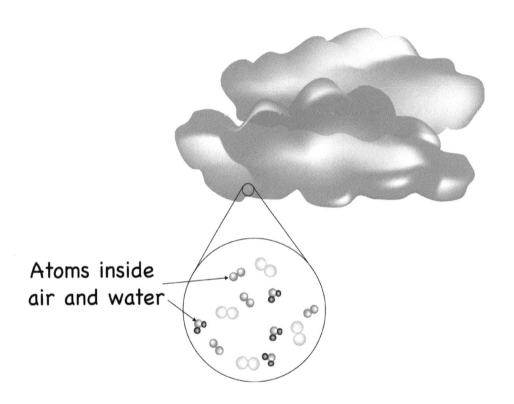

Atoms inside air and water

Carrots are orange because their atoms are arranged in a way that makes them orange.

Peas are green because their atoms are arranged in a way that makes them green.

Brussels sprouts and asparagus don't taste sweet like cherries or candy canes because the atoms inside brussels sprouts and asparagus are not arranged in a way that makes them sweet.

3.2 Types of Atoms

There are over 100 different atoms. Carbon, oxygen, and nitrogen are the names of a few of these atoms.

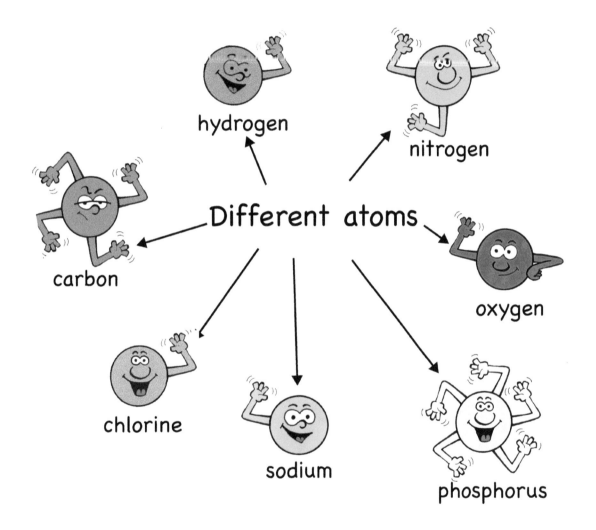

Atoms are very tiny. They are so small that you can't see them with your eyes.

Even though we can't see atoms with our eyes, we can make models of them. A model may not be exactly true, but it can help chemists understand how things work. We can make models of atoms by drawing them as dots or little balls or by giving atoms colors and shapes.

In this book, atoms are modeled as balls with "arms" to help show how atoms hook to other atoms. Even though atoms don't really have arms, it's a great way to think about how atoms hook together.

Simple Model of a Silicon Atom

3.3 Atoms Are Similar

All atoms are made of protons, neutrons, and electrons.

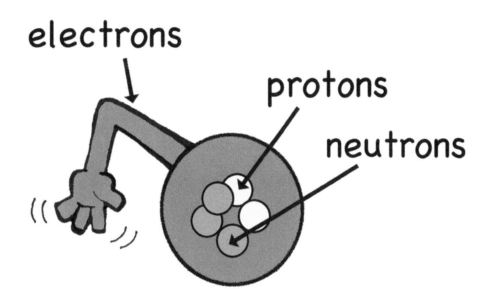

Protons, neutrons, and electrons are the basic parts of atoms. The protons and neutrons are in the center of an atom, and the electrons are on the outside.

In our model, the protons and neutrons are shown inside the ball of the atom, and the electrons are shown on the outside as the arms.

The arms in our models represent only the electrons that can help hook an atom to another atom. Some atoms have additional electrons that won't hook to another atom, and these electrons are not shown in our models.

3.4 Atoms Are Different

Atoms are different from each other because they have different numbers of protons, neutrons, and electrons.

For example, hydrogen only has one proton and one electron. It doesn't have any neutrons.

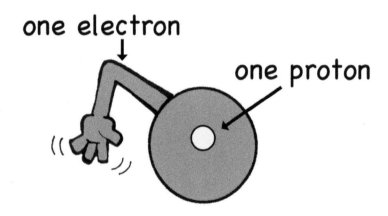

Model of a Hydrogen Atom

Carbon has six protons, six neutrons, and six electrons. However, only four of those electrons can help carbon hook to other atoms, so in our model carbon has only four arms.

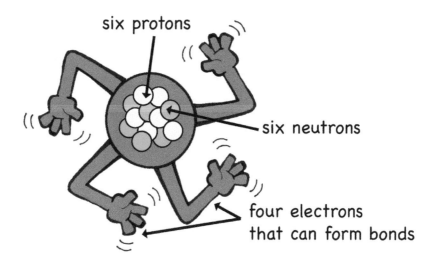

six protons

six neutrons

four electrons
that can form bonds

Model of a Carbon Atom

Uranium has 92 protons, 92 electrons, and 146 neutrons! The electrons in uranium can hook to two atoms, four atoms, or even six atoms!

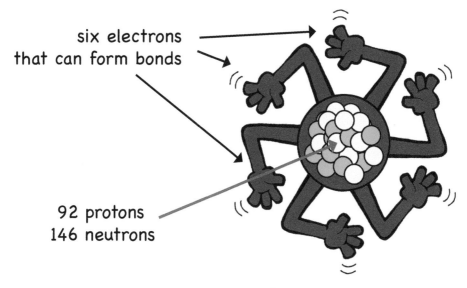

six electrons
that can form bonds

92 protons
146 neutrons

Model of a Uranium Atom

Because atoms are made of the same basic parts, all atoms are similar to each other. But because atoms are also made of different numbers of those parts, atoms are also different from each other.

Everything you can touch with your fingers, see with your eyes or smell with your nose is made of atoms. And all of these things are different from each other because their atoms are arranged in different ways.

3.5 Summary

○ Everything we touch, taste, see, or smell is made of atoms.

○ Atoms are very tiny things we can't see with our eyes. Atoms are the smallest units of matter.

○ All atoms are made of protons, neutrons, and electrons.

○ Atoms are different from each other because they have different numbers of protons, neutrons, and electrons.

3.6 Some Things to Think About

○ Which of these foods do you like to eat the most? What do you like best about each?

Asparagus

Carrots

Peas

Brussels sprouts

Green cheese

Candy canes

Cherries

○ What food is your very favorite? Besides taste, how many reasons can you think of as to why you like it?

○ How do you think making models of atoms can be helpful?

○ What do you think would happen if electrons moved to the center of an atom?

○ What do you think the world would be like if all atoms were exactly the same?

Chapter 4 Molecules

4.1 Introduction

In Chapter 3 we saw that everything is made of atoms. The Moon is made of atoms. The clouds are made of atoms. Carrots, peas, brussels sprouts, and asparagus are all made of atoms.

We also saw that all atoms are made of protons, neutrons, and electrons. We saw that atoms are different from each other when they have different numbers of protons, neutrons, and electrons.

But how do atoms make so many different things?

If we think of atoms as building blocks, we can begin to understand how atoms can make so many different things.

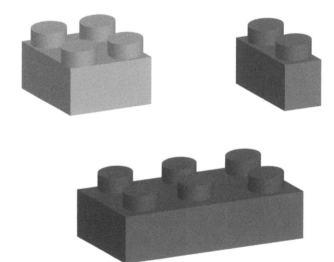

Building blocks are designed to hook to each other to make toy buildings, toy cars, or toy boats. If you look

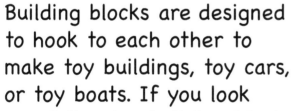

carefully at a building block, you can see that the pegs of one block fit into the holes on another block. By hooking building blocks together, different objects can be created.

In the same way that building blocks hook together to make toy cars or buildings, atoms hook to other atoms to make clouds, carrots, peas, candy canes, and the Moon!

4.2 Atoms Form Molecules

When one atom hooks to one or more other atoms, they form a molecule.

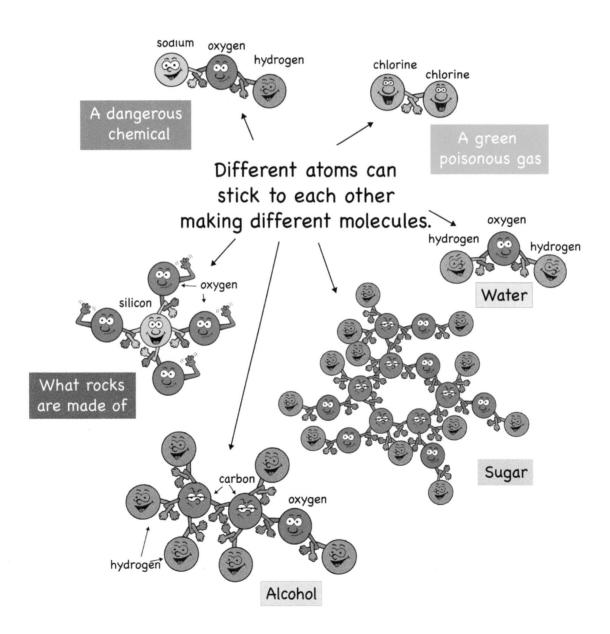

Sometimes only a couple of atoms hook together to make a molecule.

For example, table salt is made of just two atoms—sodium and chlorine.

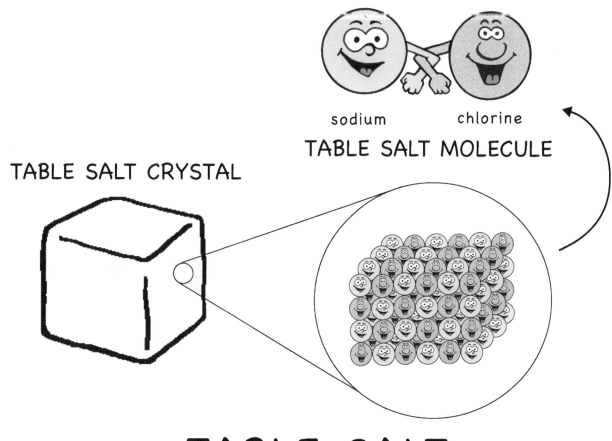

sodium   chlorine

TABLE SALT MOLECULE

TABLE SALT CRYSTAL

TABLE SALT

Water is made of three atoms—two hydrogen atoms and one oxygen atom.

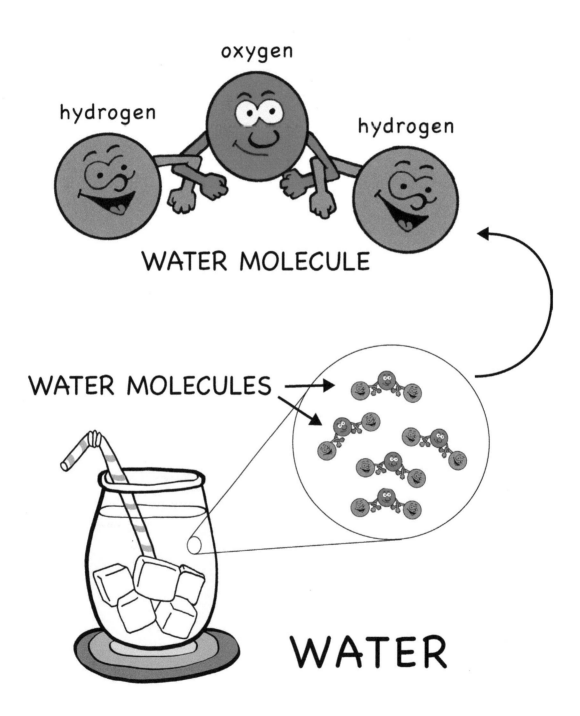

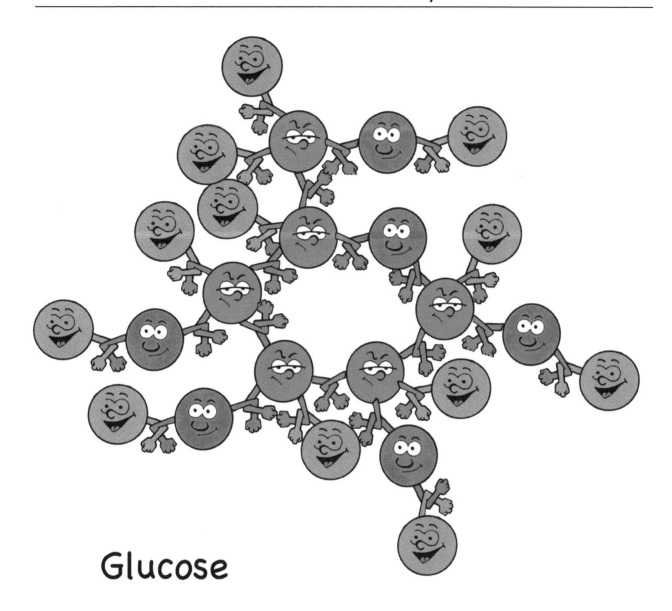

Glucose

Other molecules are made of more atoms.

Glucose, a type of sugar, is made of 24 atoms. It has
6 carbon atoms, 6 oxygen atoms, and 12 hydrogen atoms.
(Count them in the above illustration.)

Glucose is a type of carbohydrate. Carbohydrates are made
of carbon and water. Carbohydrates give your body energy.

Some of the molecules in your body, such as proteins, are made of thousands and thousands of atoms.

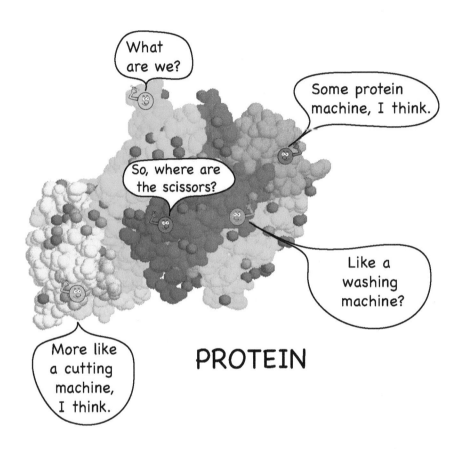

4.3 Atoms Follow Rules

Atoms hook to other atoms by following rules!

For example, each hydrogen atom can only hook to one other atom. Hydrogen cannot hook to two atoms, three atoms, or more than three atoms.

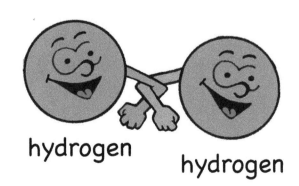

hydrogen   hydrogen

Oxygen cannot hook to more than two atoms. Nitrogen can hook to one, two, or three atoms, but nitrogen cannot hook to more than three atoms.

oxygen

nitrogen

Carbon can hook to one, two, three, or four atoms, but carbon cannot hook to more than four atoms.

Many different shapes and sizes of molecules can be made with atoms. However, atoms always obey rules when they make molecules. Following the rules means that table salt will always be table salt and sugar will always be sugar!

4.4 Summary

○ Atoms hook to other atoms to make molecules.

○ Two atoms or many atoms can hook together to form a molecule.

○ Atoms have to obey rules when making molecules.

4.5 Some Things to Think About

○ Do you think there is a limit to how many different substances can be made with atoms? Why or why not?

○ Do you think one water molecule looks the same as every other water molecule? Why or why not?

○ What do you think would happen if atoms did not have any rules to follow when hooking together? Why?

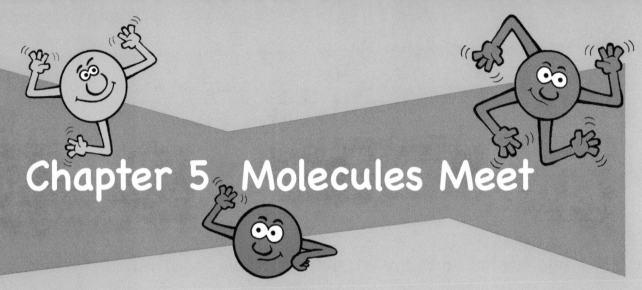

Chapter 5 Molecules Meet

5.1 When Molecules Meet

In the last chapter we saw that atoms hook together to make molecules. We also found that atoms must obey rules. Each atom hooks to other atoms in its own way.

But what happens when one molecule meets another molecule? What do they do? Do they change, or do they stay the same?

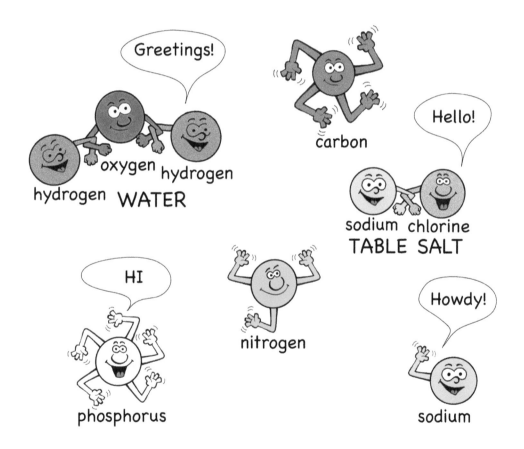

Sometimes when one molecule meets another molecule, they react. This means that something changes in the way the atoms are hooked together.

5.2 Molecules Switch Atoms

Sometimes molecules react by switching atoms (exchanging partners). In the example below, two molecules meet and trade atoms. As a result, two new molecules are made.

1 Two molecules meet.

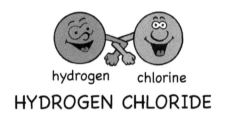

hydrogen   chlorine

HYDROGEN CHLORIDE

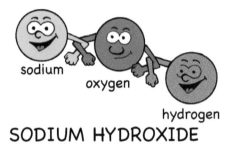

sodium   oxygen   hydrogen

SODIUM HYDROXIDE

2 The hydrogen atom and the sodium atom switch places.

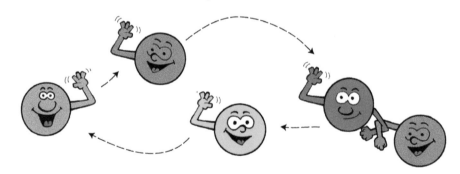

3 Two new molecules are made.

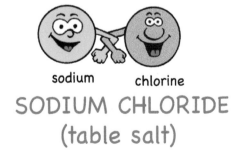

sodium   chlorine

SODIUM CHLORIDE
(table salt)

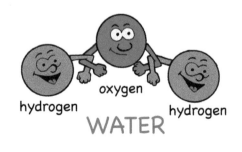

hydrogen   oxygen   hydrogen

WATER

5.3 Molecules Join Together

Sometimes when molecules meet, they join together. In this example, two chlorine atoms in a chlorine gas molecule meet two sodium atoms. The chlorine atoms and the sodium atoms combine to make table salt!

❶ Two chlorine atoms [in a chlorine gas molecule] meeting two sodium atoms.

CHLORINE GAS MOLECULE   SODIUM ATOMS

❷ The chlorine atoms join the sodium atoms to make two sodium chloride molecules [table salt].

TABLE SALT

5.4 Molecules Break Apart

Sometimes molecules simply break apart to form new molecules. In the illustration below, two water molecules break apart, and then the atoms join together in a different way to make oxygen gas and hydrogen gas.

1 Two water molecules.

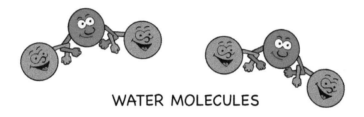

WATER MOLECULES

2 The water molecules break apart.

3 New molecules are made.

HYDROGEN GAS   OXYGEN GAS

All of these examples show how molecules and atoms react with one another. It is important to realize that in every reaction atoms are neither created nor destroyed. Atoms can rearrange themselves by combining in different ways and changing places to make new molecules, but atoms never simply appear or disappear.

5.5 Reactions Are Everywhere

When atoms join together, leave a molecule, or switch places in molecules, a chemical reaction has occurred.

There are lots of chemical reactions. They go on all the time and all around us. For example, the gasoline inside a car reacts with oxygen to provide energy for the car to move.

Reactions occur when you bake bread or cook an egg.

When you leave your metal shovel out in the rain, the red rust that forms on it is caused by a chemical reaction.

Reactions occur inside your body. When you eat a piece of cheese or drink a glass of milk, reactions occur inside your

mouth. These reactions help break down the food molecules into smaller pieces. Inside your stomach there are strong molecules that break your food down still further.

Even when you breathe, reactions inside your lungs help oxygen get into your blood so it can be carried through your body. Reactions are everywhere.

5.6 Reactions Follow Rules

Reactions also have to follow rules. Not every molecule will react with every other molecule or atom. Some molecules won't react at all. For example, the noble gases, such as neon, helium, and argon, usually don't react with any other molecules.

Some molecules react with lots of other molecules. Water will react with many different atoms and molecules. Water will even start a fire during some reactions!

5.7 We Can See Reactions

Often we can observe something happening if a reaction is occurring. Sometimes we can see bubbles. Sometimes we might see little particles form that look like sand. Sometimes the glass might change temperature in our hands if a reaction is happening. There could also be fire, an explosion, or a color change.

All of these observations tell us a reaction may be happening.

Bubbles

Fire

Particles
(like sand)

5.8 Summary

○ When atoms get rearranged, a chemical reaction has occurred.

○ Atoms can switch places, join together, or separate from each other during a chemical reaction.

○ In a chemical reaction atoms rearrange but are never created or destroyed.

○ Reactions occur everywhere.

○ We may be seeing a reaction take place when there are bubbles, color changes, or temperature changes.

5.9 Some Things to Think About

○ Which is your favorite atom? Why?

  carbon

  nitrogen

  sodium

  phosphorus

  hydrogen

  oxygen

○ Do you think an atom in one molecule can switch places with any atom in any other molecule? Why or why not?

○ Chlorine is poisonous but you can eat table salt that has chlorine in it. What do you think happens that makes it possible for you to eat table salt that has chlorine in it?

○ What rules do you think oxygen atoms and hydrogen atoms follow when they make a water molecule? What rules do you think oxygen atoms and hydrogen atoms follow when they make oxygen or hydrogen gas?

○ What do you think would happen if there were no chemical reactions in your body?

○ Why do you think some molecules won't react with some atoms?

○ What have you observed that showed that a chemical reaction was probably taking place?

Chapter 6 Acids and Bases

6.1 Introduction

When atoms and molecules meet, they can trade places, join together, or separate from each other. A chemical reaction happens when atoms or molecules meet and any of these changes take place. A chemical reaction is one of the events chemists measure with tools.

In this chapter we will look at some special kinds of chemical reactions. These reactions are called acid-base reactions. Acid-base reactions are easy for chemists to study with some basic tools.

6.2 Acids and Bases Are Different

Have you ever noticed that when you bite a lemon it tastes sour and makes your cheeks pucker?

Have you ever tasted mineral water or baking soda water? They are not sour like a lemon. They are bitter or salty.

Have you ever noticed that soap is very slippery in your fingers, but lemon juice and vinegar are not?

The molecules inside a lemon are different from the molecules inside baking soda water or mineral water. Lemons have molecules in them called acids. It is the acid in lemons that gives them their sour taste.

Baking soda water and soap contain molecules that are called bases. Bases often make things feel slippery or taste bitter.

6.3 H and OH Groups

Acids and bases are different from each other in many ways. This is because a base is a different kind of molecule than an acid. Acids and bases are different because they have different atom groups.

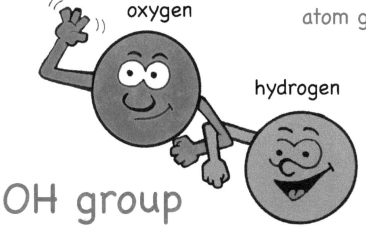

oxygen

hydrogen

OH group

A base has an OH group [say "O" "H" group]. An OH group is just an oxygen atom and a hydrogen atom together.

Most common acids have an H group [say "H" group]. An H group is just a hydrogen atom.

H group

We can see in the next picture that sodium hydroxide (a base) has an OH group and hydrogen chloride (an acid) has an H group.

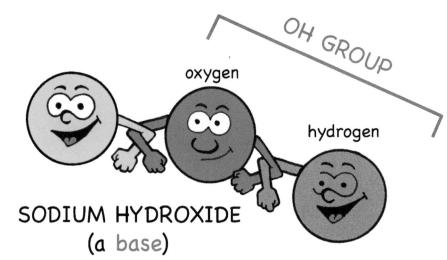

SODIUM HYDROXIDE
(a base)

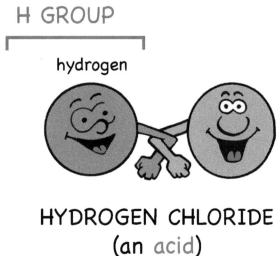

HYDROGEN CHLORIDE
(an acid)

6.4 Both Are Important

Both acids and bases are very important. They are needed in lots of very useful chemical reactions. You have a strong acid inside your stomach to break down your food. Without the acid in our stomachs, we could not digest our food.

Acids are also found in batteries, lemons, oranges, grapes, and even soda pop.

These things have acids in them.

Bases are found in lots of cleaners, like window cleaner, bathroom cleaner, and soap. They are also found in some foods like bananas and dates. Bases are even used to make your stomach feel better! We'll see why in the next chapter.

These things
have bases
in them.

6.5 Observing Acids and Bases

Chemists can use basic tools to see an acid-base reaction. Some acids and bases give off heat or explode when they react. Other times we cannot tell when an acid-base reaction happens. When we can't see an acid-base reaction, we can put something into the acid-base mixture that will show us that the reaction is taking place. This "something" is called an indicator because it indicates, or tells us, something is happening or has happened.

Indicators

We use different kinds of indicators all the time. Stop lights indicate when we can go or when we should stop. When we turn on the oven, an indicator tells us when it is hot enough. A thermometer is an indicator. It can tell when your body has a fever. Indicators are also used in chemistry.

An acid-base indicator tells us whether we have an acid or a base. There are different kinds of acid-base indicators. A simple acid-base indicator is red cabbage juice! Red cabbage juice turns pink with acids and green with bases.

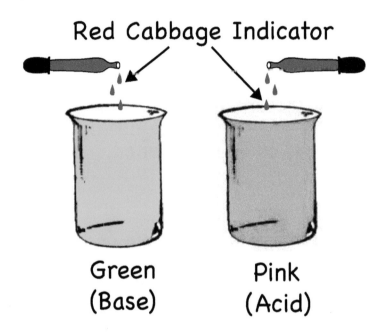

Red Cabbage Indicator

Green
(Base)

Pink
(Acid)

6.6 Summary

○ Acids taste sour.

○ Bases taste bitter and are slippery.

○ Acids have an H group, and bases have an OH group.

○ Acids and bases are found everywhere—in batteries, in your stomach, in household cleaners, and even in bananas and lemons!

○ An acid-base indicator tells us whether we have an acid or a base.

6.7 Some Things to Think About

○ What is your favorite acid-base reaction?

Watching baking soda and vinegar react

Watching lemon juice, baking soda, and soap react

Making soap

Cleaning rust off a yard tool with vinegar

Watching vinegar and milk react

○ Do you think bubble bath is an acid or a base? Why?

○ How would you describe the difference between an H group and an OH group?

○ What is your favorite basic food?

Carrot juice

Bananas

Dried figs

Raisins

Green beans

○ What are some indicators in your house?

Chapter 7   Acids and Bases React

7.1 When Acids and Bases Meet

In the last chapter we learned about two different kinds of molecules—acids and bases. We saw that acids and bases are found in lots of different things. Acids are in batteries, lemons, and even soda pop. Bases are in soap, window cleaner, and bananas too.

What happens when acids and bases meet? When molecules meet, sometimes they react. Do acids and bases react when they meet?

1. An acid and a base meet.

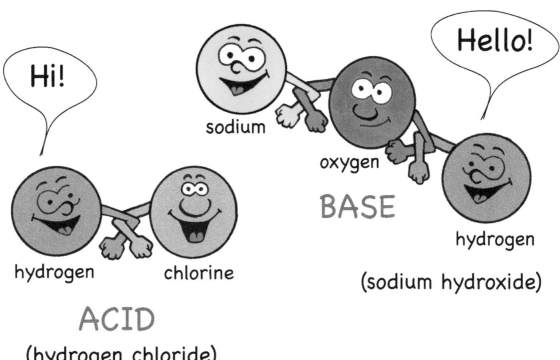

7.2 Acid-Base Reactions

In fact, they do! Acids and bases make a special kind of reaction called an acid-base reaction. When an acid and a base meet, the atoms in the acid exchange with the atoms in the base.

After they meet, some atoms leave their molecules.

2. The atoms leave their molecules.

Next, the atoms that left their molecules go to the other molecules and "make new friends."

3. The atoms make new friends.

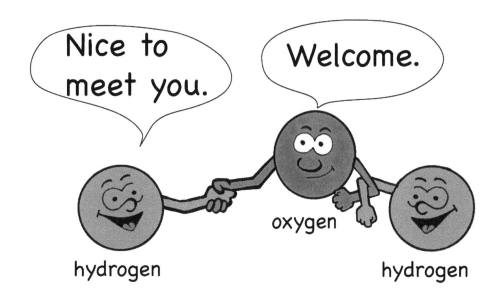

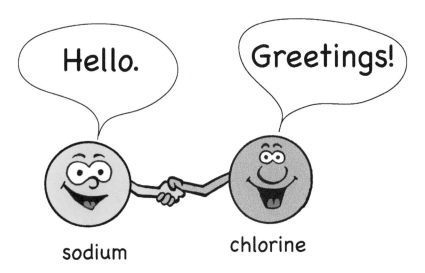

Now two new molecules have been made. The new molecules for this reaction are water and table salt (sodium chloride).

4. Two new molecules are made.

hydrogen   oxygen   hydrogen

Water

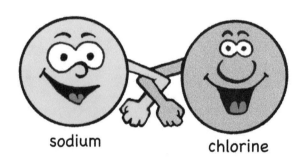

sodium   chlorine

Table Salt
(sodium chloride)

The acids and bases are no longer acids and bases. When they react, they become other kinds of molecules, such as salt and water.

7.3 Important Acid-Base Reactions

Acid-base reactions are very important. For example, your stomach has acid in it. This acid is necessary for digesting your food. Sometimes there is too much acid. When this happens, your stomach hurts. The medicine your mom or

dad may give you is a base. It reacts with the acid in your stomach, turning it into a salt and water. That makes your stomach stop hurting.

7.4 Summary

○ Acids and bases react with each other in acid-base reactions.

○ When an acid and a base meet in an acid-base reaction, atoms in the acid exchange with atoms in the base.

○ Many acid-base reactions make salts and water.

○ Acid-base reactions are very important.

7.5 Some Things to Think About

○ Have you ever added vinegar to baking soda? If so, can you describe what happened?

○ How would you describe an acid-base reaction to your friend?

○ What is your favorite remedy to take when your tummy hurts?

   pink antacid

   baking soda and water

   vinegar and water

   clear soda

   pickle juice

Chapter 8   Mixtures

8.1 Mixing

Have you ever put water and sand together in a pail? What did you get? A mud pie maybe!

Have you ever made a real pie, like lemon pie? If you have, you probably added eggs and flour, some table salt and oil, and maybe some water. What happened when you added all these things together? You probably mixed them with a spoon or a mixer.

In either case, what you ended up with is a mixture.

A mixture of sand and water or a mixture of eggs, oil, lemon, and water—both mud pies and lemon pies are mixtures.

8.2 Mixtures

You can make a mixture of blocks and rocks. You can make a mixture of rocks and sand. You can make a mixture of sugar and cinnamon and put it on your toast! All of these are called mixtures because all of these are made of more than one thing mixed together.

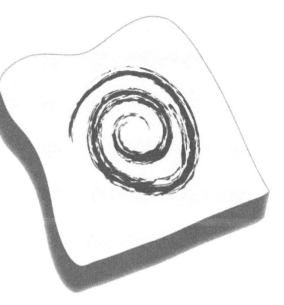

8.3 Some Mixtures Dissolve

Have you ever wondered why table salt disappears in water, but sand does not? Have you ever noticed that sugar disappears in water but not in oil or butter? When table salt or sugar disappear in water, we say they dissolve.

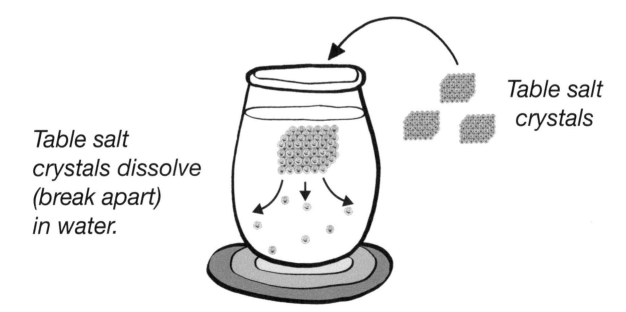

Table salt crystals dissolve (break apart) in water.

Table salt crystals

Some things will dissolve in water and some things will not dissolve. What makes some things dissolve and other things not dissolve?

8.4 Dissolving

As with everything else, it's the molecules in table salt and sugar that determine whether or not they will dissolve.

Molecules have to follow rules for dissolving or not dissolving, just like they have to follow rules for reacting or not reacting.

The main "rule" for dissolving is:

Like dissolves like.

This means, for example, that molecules that are "like" water *will* dissolve in water and molecules that are "not like" water *will not* dissolve in water.

This doesn't mean that the molecules have to be identical or *exactly* alike, they just need to have a few things in common.

Water

For example, what makes some molecules "like" water? Acid molecules have an H group (one hydrogen atom) and bases have an OH group (an oxygen atom and a hydrogen atom). If we look carefully at water, we see that it has BOTH an OH group and an H group! This is one of the things that makes water very special.

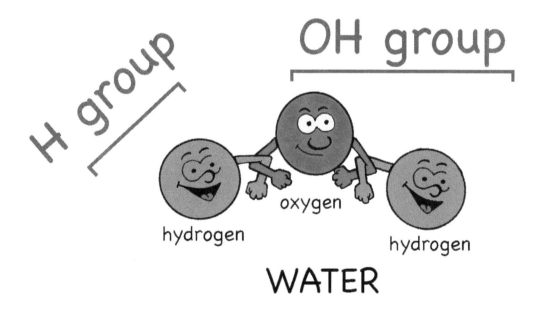

H group

OH group

hydrogen

oxygen

hydrogen

WATER

It is the OH group that makes molecules dissolve in water. Bases that have OH groups are "like" water and will dissolve in water. Other molecules, like alcohol, which is not a base but still has an OH group, will also dissolve in water.

Sugar is "like" water because sugar also has OH groups. Can you count how many OH groups sugar has?

1 Alcohol, sugar, and sodium hydroxide are "like" water—they have OH groups.

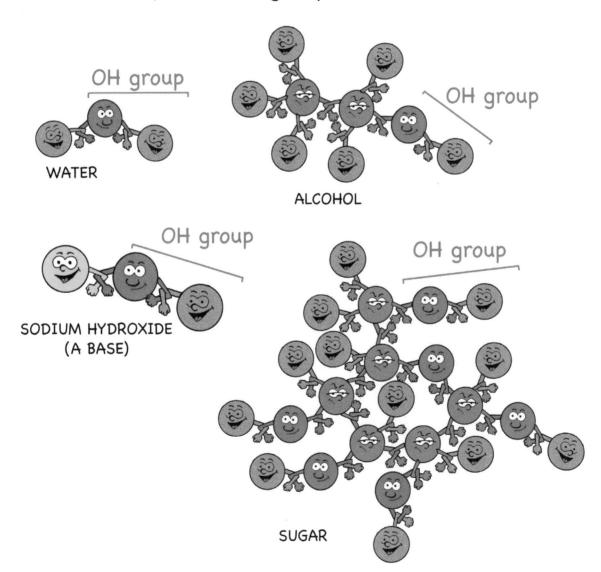

It's not just OH groups that make some things dissolve in water. For example, salt doesn't have OH groups like sugar, alcohol, and bases do, but salt dissolves in water. Salt dissolves in water because the water molecules break the salt molecules into pieces that mix with water.

2 Salt will dissolve in water.

First the salt breaks apart...

...and then the salt atoms mix
with the water molecules.

Oil, grease, and butter are not like water, so none of these will dissolve in water. Look carefully at the drawing that illustrates the type of molecule found in oil, grease, and butter. Can you tell why it is not like water?

3   Oil, grease, and butter are not like water.

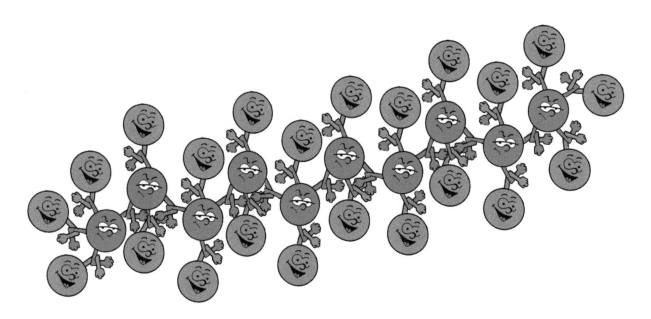

TYPE OF MOLECULE FOUND IN OIL, GREASE, AND BUTTER

8.5 Soap

Soap makes things like butter and grease dissolve in water. Soap can do this because the molecules that make up soap are a little like water and a little like oil.

4   Soap has an "oil-like" part and a "water-like" part.

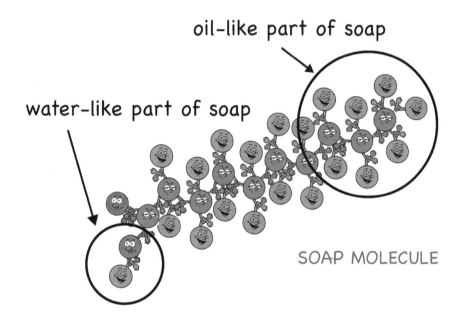

oil-like part of soap

water-like part of soap

SOAP MOLECULE

In a mixture of oil, soap, and water, the oily part of soap will dissolve in the oil, and the watery part of soap will dissolve in the water.

5 The "oil-like" part of soap dissolves in the oil, and the "water-like" part dissolves in the water.

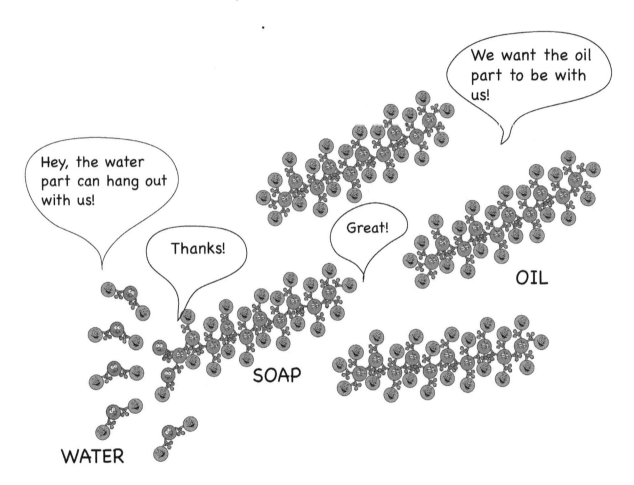

WATER, SOAP, AND OIL MIXTURE

Because the oil dissolves in the oily part of soap, and the watery part of soap dissolves in the water, a small droplet of oil and soap forms. In this way, the oil is "trapped" by the soap and water inside this little droplet.

This droplet can then be washed away by the water. This is how soap washes the grease off your hands!

6 Droplet of oil molecules and soap surrounded by water molecules.

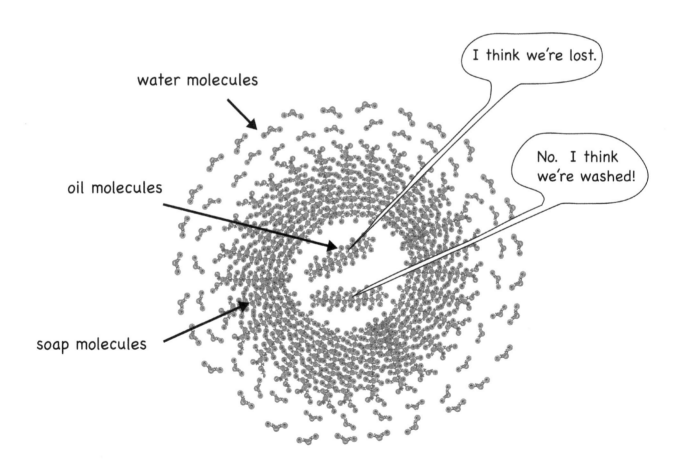

8.6 Summary

○ Mud pies and lemon pies are mixtures.

○ A mixture is anything that has two or more types of items in it.

○ Some mixtures dissolve. Others do not.

○ Dissolving depends on the kind of molecules in the mixture. Molecules that are "like" each other dissolve. Molecules that are "not like" each other will not dissolve.

○ Soap is like both water and oil. This means that soap can make oil "dissolve" in water.

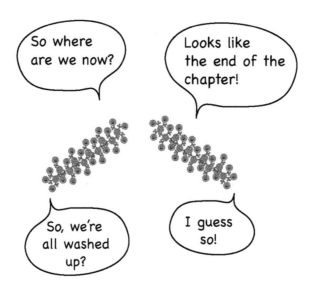

8.7 Some Things to Think About

○ What is your favorite mixture to eat?

○ What are some things that you like to mix together?

○ Take a glass of water and mix a spoonful of salt into it. What happens?

  Take a glass of water and mix a spoonful of sugar into it. What happens?

  Take a glass of water and mix a spoonful of peas into it. What happens?

○ Do you think vegetable oil will dissolve in water? Why or why not?

○ What do you think determines whether one substance will dissolve in another?

○ What do you think would happen if soap was only "like water" and did not have a part that is "like oil"?

Chapter 9   Un-mixing

9.1 Un-mixing

In the last chapter we learned about mixtures, but how do we get things that are mixed to "un-mix?" Can we get the water and sand to "un-mix" from a mud pie? Can we get the eggs, sugar, water, and lemons to "un-mix" from a lemon pie?

Try to think of ways to "un-mix" a mud pie. What if you let the mud pie bake in the sun? What happens to the water? What happens to the sand?

9.2 Evaporation

You may know that the water "disappears" from the mud pie and the sand stays behind. We say that the water has evaporated. Evaporation is one way to "un-mix," or separate, mixtures that have water in them.

What happens if we leave the lemon pie to bake in the sun? Will the lemon pie "un-mix"? The water will evaporate, but what happens to the eggs, sugar, and lemons? They do not evaporate. In fact, they stay behind and we have a not-so-tasty lemon mess!

9.3 Sorting By Hand

Sometimes we can "un-mix" things, and sometimes we cannot. The mud pie can be "un-mixed," by the sun, but the lemon pie cannot.

Large things are usually easy to "un-mix." Even though when your mom tells you to clean your room, the large pile of toys may seem impossible to "un-mix"—with some work, it can be done.

All of the toys are easy to pick up because they are large. They can be picked up with your hands and put into separate bins or boxes.

9.4 Using Tools

What about a pile of sand? The sand cannot be easily picked up because each piece of sand is very small. It would take hours to pick up all of the sand by hand!

Fortunately a tool can be used. Can you think of a tool for picking up sand and "un-mixing" it from your carpet?

That's right—a vacuum cleaner! A vacuum cleaner can be used as a tool for "un-mixing."

In fact, tools are used all the time to "un-mix" things that are hard to "un-mix" with your hands. For example, sieves or colanders are used to separate hot spaghetti or hot potatoes from boiling water.

9.5 Using "Tricks"

There are other tools and other ways to "un-mix" mixtures of small things. What about molecules that you can't even see? Are there ways to separate molecules?

There are! In fact, scientists use a trick called chromatography to separate molecules. Using chromatography, you can un-mix many different kinds of molecules.

One type of chromatography is called paper chromatography. With paper chromatography, a piece of paper is used to separate small things like molecules. You can use paper chromatography to separate the small molecules that are in ink or dye, or even the molecules found in a colored flower!

Paper Chromatography

Ink colors "un-mixing" on the paper

Mixture of different colored ink

paper

Dish

Ink crawls up the paper

9.6 Summary

○ The sand and water in a mud pie can be "un-mixed" by evaporating away the water.

○ Some mixtures, such as lemon pies, cannot be easily "un-mixed."

○ Mixtures of large things are easier to "un-mix" than mixtures of smaller things.

○ Tools, like vacuum cleaners and sieves, can be used to "un-mix" some mixtures.

○ A trick called chromatography can be used to separate molecules.

9.7 Some Things to Think About

○ What steps would you take to make a chocolate cake? Do you think you could un-mix the chocolate cake that you made? If so, how would you do it? If not, why not?

○ What are some times when you have noticed that water has evaporated?

○ Make a list of some mixtures of objects that you have sorted by using your hands.

○ Think of some tools you could use to un-mix mixtures. Make a list!

○ Do you think you could use any kind of paper to do paper chromatography? Why or why not?

Chapter 10   Molecular Chains

10.1 Chains of Molecules

Sugar molecules hook together to form a long chain. These long chains of sugar molecules are called carbohydrates.

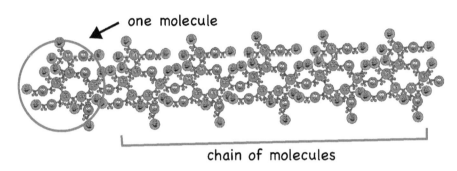

one molecule

chain of molecules

CARBOHYDRATE

There are other kinds of long chains not made of sugar molecules. Long chains can be made out of many different kinds of molecules. In general, long chains of molecules are called polymers.

Polymer

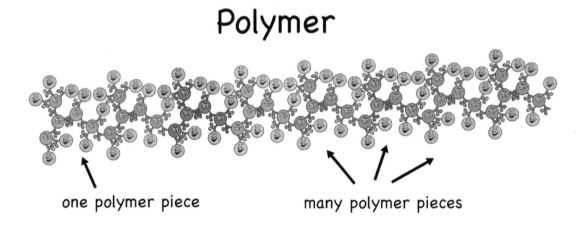

one polymer piece   many polymer pieces

Polymers are everywhere! Almost anywhere you look, you can find polymers. Your clothes, your toys, your food, and your hair are all made of polymers!

10.2 Different Polymers

Plastics are polymers. Your toy car and parts of your dad's car are made of polymers.

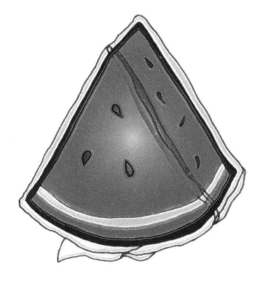

The plastic wrap you put over your food is made of polymers.

The plastic cup you drink from and the plastic pen you write with are made of polymers.

Rubber is also a polymer. The rubber hose outside in the garden, a rubber ball, and the rubber boots you wear on rainy days are all made of polymers.

Styrofoam is a polymer. The packing peanuts that come with your new chemistry kit are made of polymers. The Styrofoam cup that holds your dad's coffee or your lemonade is made of polymers.

Your clothing is also made of polymers. Cotton fibers, nylon fibers, polyester, and wool are all polymers. Polymers are everywhere!

10.3 Polymers Can Change

How can polymers make so many different things if they are all just long molecules?

Because different polymers have different properties (like being sticky or stiff), many different things can be made with polymers.

Sometimes long chains of polymers slide up and down next to each other. Polymers that are like this, such as glue and natural rubber, can be sticky.

Sometimes long chains of polymers are hooked together and can't slide up and down next to each other. Polymers like this can be hard or stiff and not sticky.

It is possible to change the properties of polymers by using chemicals or heat to cause a chemical reaction. For example, egg whites are made of polymers. When you cook an egg, you change the properties of the polymers inside the egg. The egg whites change from a clear, sticky liquid to a firm, white solid when you cook them. The polymers inside the egg whites change their properties because the heat causes a chemical reaction.

10.4 Summary

○ Polymers are long chains of smaller molecules that are hooked together.

○ Polymers are everywhere! Plastics, rubber, Styrofoam, and clothing are all made of polymers.

○ Different polymers give objects different properties. Some polymers make things soft, and some polymers make things hard or stiff.

○ You can change the properties of a polymer by use of chemical reactions or heat.

10.5 Some Things to Think About

○ What do you think Earth would be like if molecules could not hook together into long chains?

○ Do you think YOU are made of polymers? Why or why not?

○ Why do you think different polymers have different properties?

Chapter 11   Food and Taste

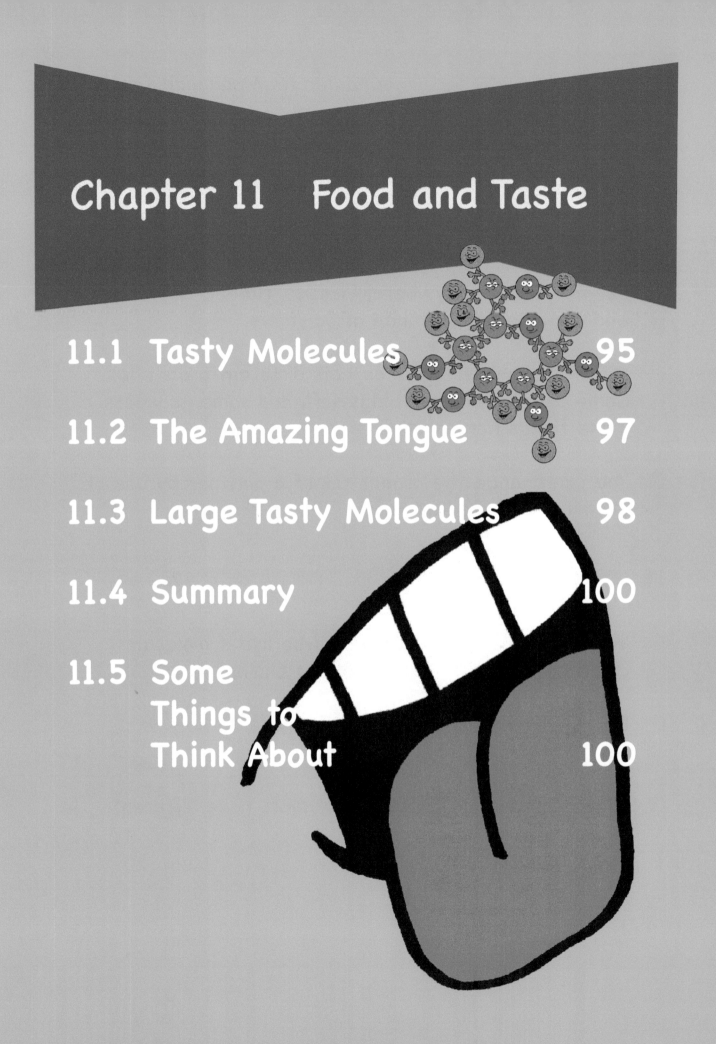

11.1 Tasty Molecules

Now you know why vinegar and lemons taste sour—they're acids! And why mineral water and soda water taste bitter—they're bases! Have you ever wondered why salt tastes salty and sugar tastes sweet?

We have learned that everything around us is made of atoms, and atoms combine to make molecules. The food we eat is made of molecules, but not all of the food we eat tastes the same. Why? Different molecules in different foods make foods taste different.

1. Acid molecules found in soda pop...

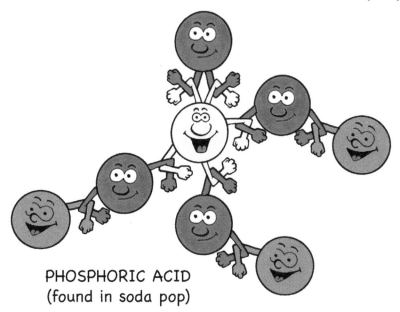

PHOSPHORIC ACID
(found in soda pop)

...make soda pop taste sour*.

(*soda pop also has lots and lots of sugar in it, so it also tastes very sweet.)

2. Acid molecules in vinegar...

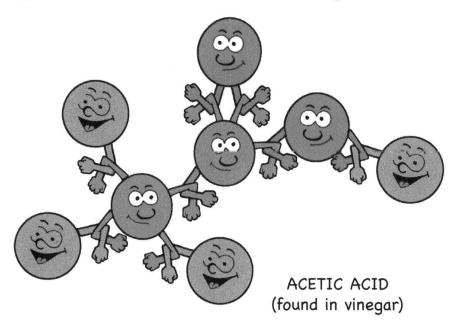

ACETIC ACID
(found in vinegar)

... make vinegar taste sour.

We have already seen that sour foods often have an acid in them. Lemons, vinegar, and grapefruit have acid in them. When you eat foods with acid in them, your tongue tells your brain "sour."

Foods that have salt in them taste salty. Salt molecules look very different from acid molecules. Remember that table salt has a sodium atom and a chlorine atom hooked together. When you eat foods with salt in them, your tongue tells your brain "salty."

sodium   chlorine

SODIUM CHLORIDE
(table salt)

11.2 The Amazing Tongue

Your tongue is designed to tell your brain what kind of molecules are in your food. It can sense acids, bases, salt, sugar, and many other molecules. The tongue is essentially a tool your body uses to detect certain atoms and molecules.

For example, foods that taste sweet have sugar in them. A sugar molecule looks different from a salt molecule or an acid molecule. A sugar molecule is larger, has more atoms in it, and some of the atoms are hooked together in a ring. When you eat a piece of candy, your tongue tells your brain "sweet" because your tongue senses sugar.

GLUCOSE (a sugar)

Your tongue can tell the difference between a salt molecule, an acid molecule, and a sugar molecule.

Your tongue is a remarkable indicator.

Remember from Chapter 6 that an acid-base indicator tells the difference between acids and bases. There are lots of man-made indicators, like acid-base indicators, thermometers, and stop lights, but there are no indicators as intricately designed as your own tongue!

11.3 Large Tasty Molecules

Even though your tongue is an amazing indicator, your tongue can't taste all molecules. For example, a raw potato doesn't exactly taste sweet, salty, bitter, or sour, but something in between. In fact, a potato is made mostly of sugar molecules, but your tongue can't taste the sugar molecules in a raw potato because the molecules are hooked together in long chains called carbohydrates.

one glucose molecule

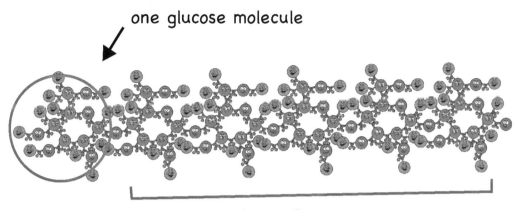

chain of glucose molecules

CARBOHYDRATE

Many different foods have carbohydrates. Bread, pasta, potatoes, and many fruits have carbohydrates in them. Carbohydrates are important molecules for your body. Because carbohydrates are made of sugar molecules, they provide the energy your body needs to ride a bike or climb a tree!

11.4 Summary

○ Foods taste different because foods are made of different molecules.

○ Your tongue is an amazing indicator that can tell the difference between salts, acids, bases, and sugars.

○ Carbohydrates are long chains of sugar molecules.

○ Your tongue can't taste sugar molecules in foods that contain carbohydrates if the carbohydrates are hooked together in long chains of molecules.

11.5 Some Things to Think About

○ What is your favorite salty food?
What is your favorite sweet food?
What other types of flavors can you taste?

○ Why do you think taste is important?
What would your life be like if you couldn't taste anything?

○ Do you think your tongue can tell the difference between a spoonful of mashed potatoes and a slice of raw potato? Why or why not?

Chapter 12   Molecules in Your Body

12.1 Special Polymers

In Chapter 10 we looked at long chains of molecules called polymers. We learned that plastics, rubber, clothing, and food are all made of polymers.

Did you know that many of the molecules inside your body are also polymers? There are many different polymers inside your body. We will learn about two of them.

One very special kind of polymer is called a protein.

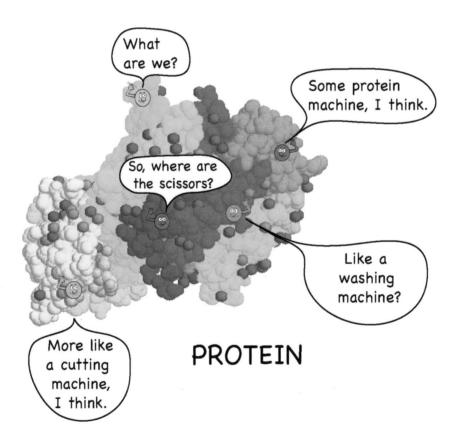

PROTEIN

A protein is a long chain of small molecules hooked together and often folded up into a special shape. It is the special shape of this folded chain of molecules that helps proteins do amazing things.

12.2 Proteins—Tiny Machines

Proteins are tiny machines inside your body that perform incredible tasks. In fact, proteins do almost all of the work inside your body.

Some proteins glue other molecules together.

Some proteins cut other molecules.

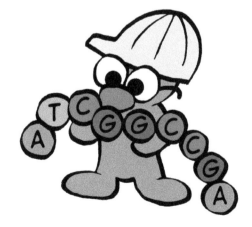

Some proteins copy other molecules and some proteins "read" other molecules.

Some proteins move other proteins or molecules from place to place.

Proteins do an amazing number of different jobs inside your body.

12.3 DNA—A Blueprint

One of the molecules that proteins read, cut, paste, and carry is called DNA. DNA is also a polymer.

DNA

DNA is a very special molecule. It is not just any ordinary polymer. DNA is special because DNA carries your genetic code. A genetic code is like a set of instructions. Your genetic code determines if you will have brown hair or blonde hair. Your genetic code tells whether you will have green eyes or blue eyes, or whether you will have light skin or dark skin. The genetic code carried by your DNA is essentially the blueprint for your body.

Everyone has a different and unique genetic code, or blueprint. You get your blueprint from your parents, and they got their blueprint from their parents. Your parent's parents got their blueprint from their parents, and so on. Your blueprint tells what you will look like and how tall you may grow, but your blueprint doesn't tell everything about you.

Where you live, what you eat, what you do, and even what you think make you unique and not like any other person who ever lived or who ever will live! Even identical twins who have identical DNA are different from each other. You are more than just your DNA. You are uniquely designed in every way.

12.4 Summary

○ There are polymers in our bodies.

○ Some polymers are called proteins. Proteins are tiny machines that glue, cut, copy, and carry molecules in your body.

○ Some polymers are called DNA. DNA carries the genetic code.

○ Your body is an amazing design of large and small molecules, polymers, and genetic information. You are uniquely designed.

12.5 Some Things to Think About

○ Why do you think it might be important to have lots of different kinds of proteins in your body?

○ What do you think happens when proteins glue molecules together?

○ Why do you think proteins need to move other proteins and molecules from one place to another?

○ Why do you think proteins need to copy other molecules in the body?

○ If you look at your family members, what features can you see that are shared and what features are different?

Glossary–Index

acid (AA-sed) • a type of molecule that has a sour taste, 52-58, 61-65, 71, 95, 96, 97, 98

acid-base indicator (AA-sed BASE IN-duh-kay-tur) • something that tells us whether a substance is an acid or a base, 58, 98

acid-base reaction (AA-sed BASE ree-AK-shun) • a special kind of chemical reaction that occurs when an acid and a base meet, 52-58, 61-65

advanced tool • a complicated tool; an instrument, 13, 15

alchemist (AL-kem-ist) • an early chemist who explored different chemicals and how they react, 12-13

alcohol (AL-kuh-hawl) • a molecule that is not a base but has an OH group and dissolves in water, 72

alembic (uh-LEM-bik) • an apparatus used in some experiments that involve liquids, 13

argon (AR-gahn) • a type of atom, 47

atom (AA-tum) • the smallest unit of matter, 6, 7, 12, 19-28, 31-38, 52-54, 62-63, 71, 73, 97

balance (BAA-lens) • a tool used to measure weight, 14

base • a type of molecule that has a bitter taste and feels slippery, 52-58, 61-65, 71-73, 95, 97, 98

basic tool • a simple tool, 13-14, 52, 57

beaker (BEE-kuhr) • a type of measuring cup used in a chemistry lab, 14

Buchner (BUCK-ner) **flask** • a type of container that has a neck, 16

carbohydrate (car-boe-HYE-drait) • a long chain of sugar molecules that is made of carbon and water and is used by the body for energy, 35, 88, 98-99

carbon (CAR-buhn) • a type of atom, 23, 27, 35, 38

chemical process (KEH-muh-kul PRAH-ses) • any activity that involves chemistry, 3

chemical reaction (KEH-muh-kul ree-ACK-shun) • occurs when atoms join together, leave a molecule, or switch places, 12, 41-48, 52, 55, 92

chemistry (KEH-muh-stree) • the investigation of what physical things are made of and the ways in which they change—the study of matter, 2-9

chlorine (KLAW-reen) • a type of atom, 33, 43, 96

chromatography (kroe-muh-TAH-gruh-fee) • a method of separating a mixture, 84

molecule (MAH-li-kyool) • two or more atoms hooked together, 31-38, 41-48, 52-53, 61-64, 70-77, 84-85, 88-91, 95-99, 102-105

neon (NEE-on) • a type of atom, 47

neutron (NOO-tron) • one of the 3 basic parts of an atom; found in the center of the atom, 25-27, 31

nitrogen (NYE-truh-jun) • a type of atom, 23, 37

noble gas • a type of atom that doesn't usually react with other atoms or molecules, 47

OH group [pronounced: "O" "H" group] • an oxygen atom and a hydrogen atom joined together; found in a base, 53-54, 62, 71-73

oxygen (OCK-si-jun) • a type of atom, 23, 34, 35, 37, 44, 45, 47, 53, 71

oxygen (OCK-si-jun) **gas** • a molecule made of 2 oxygen atoms, 15, 44

paper chromatography (kroh-muh-TAH-gruh-fee) • a method of separating a mixture by using paper, 84-85

particle (PAR-ti-kul) • in a chemical reaction, a small, solid piece of matter that results from the reaction, 48

pelican (PE-li-kun) • an apparatus used in some experiments that involve liquids, 13

phosphoric acid • (fas-FAWR-ik AA-sed) • a molecule found in soda pop, 95

phosphorus (FAS-fuh-rus) • a type of atom, 23

polymer (PA-luh-mer) • a long chain of molecules, 88-92, 102-105

property (PRAH-per-tee) [plural, **properties**] • a quality or characteristic, 91, 92

protein (PROE-teen) • a long chain of small molecules hooked together that are found in the body and do special jobs, 36, 102-104

proton (PROE-tahn) • one of the 3 basic parts of an atom; found in the center of the atom, 25, 26,27, 31

react (ree-AKT) • in chemistry, when molecules meet and join together or break apart, 41, 42, 70

reaction (ree-AK-shun) • in chemistry, a chemical reaction, 12, 41-48, 52, 55, 57, 61-65, 92

scale • a tool used to measure weight, 14

sense • to perceive or become aware of, 97

separate (SE-puh-rait) • for mixtures, to remove one or more substances from a mixture, 81, 84

sieve (SIV) • a device that has a screen or holes in it; separates mixtures by allowing smaller particles through while keeping larger ones behind, 84

soap • a base that has an "oil-like" part and a "water-like" part, 53, 56, 61, 75-77

sodium (SOE-dee-um) • a type of atom, 33, 42, 43, 54, 61, 64, 72, 96

sodium chloride (SOE-dee-um KLAW-ride) • table salt, 42, 64

sodium hydroxide (SOE-dee-um hye-DROCK-side) • a base, 54, 61, 72

specialized (SPE-shuh-liezd) • made for a specific use, 15, 16

table salt • a substance made of 2 atoms—sodium and chlorine; sodium chloride, 33, 38, 43, 64, 69, 70, 73, 96

temperature (TEM-per-chur) • a measure of heat, 48

tool • a device used to perform a job, 12-16, 52, 57, 83-84, 97

uranium (yoo-RAY-nee-um) • a type of atom, 27

vacuum (VA-kyoom) cleaner • a device used to pick up small particles by use of suction, 84

water • a molecule made from 2 hydrogen atoms and one oxygen atom, 13, 34, 35, 42, 44, 48, 64, 68-77, 81-82

More REAL SCIENCE-4-KIDS Books
by Rebecca W. Keller, PhD

Building Blocks Series yearlong study program — each Student Textbook has accompanying Laboratory Notebook, Teacher's Manual, Lesson Plan, Study Notebook, Quizzes, and Graphics Package

Exploring the Building Blocks of Science Book K (Activity Book)
Exploring the Building Blocks of Science Book 1
Exploring the Building Blocks of Science Book 2
Exploring the Building Blocks of Science Book 3
Exploring the Building Blocks of Science Book 4
Exploring the Building Blocks of Science Book 5
Exploring the Building Blocks of Science Book 6
Exploring the Building Blocks of Science Book 7
Exploring the Building Blocks of Science Book 8

Focus Series unit study program — each title has a Student Textbook with accompanying Laboratory Notebook, Teacher's Manual, Lesson Plan, Study Notebook, Quizzes, and Graphics Package

Focus On Elementary Chemistry
Focus On Elementary Biology
Focus On Elementary Physics
Focus On Elementary Geology
Focus On Elementary Astronomy

Focus On Middle School Chemistry
Focus On Middle School Biology
Focus On Middle School Physics
Focus On Middle School Geology
Focus On Middle School Astronomy

Focus On High School Chemistry

Super Simple Science Experiments

21 Super Simple Chemistry Experiments
21 Super Simple Biology Experiments
21 Super Simple Physics Experiments
21 Super Simple Geology Experiments
21 Super Simple Astronomy Experiments
101 Super Simple Science Experiments

Note: A few titles may still be in production.

Gravitas Publications Inc.
www.gravitaspublications.com
www.realscience4kids.com